CLUELESS

The Diary of a First-Time Girl Mom

**BY: BRITTNEY
"O.G NEWNEW"
BRESTON**

INTRO	1
JUST A LITTLE HISTORY	3
THE FOUNDATION	7
THE MAKING OF A GIRL MOM	16
THE BEGINNING OF ACCEPTANCE	46
WHAT IS LOVE?	54
RAISING YOUR SONS & DAUGHTERS EQUALLY	57
FEAUX REASONS CLUE WILL NOT BE CLUELESS	64
CONCLUSION	74

INTRO

As a mom of four boys and a tom-boy myself, having a girl was the last thing on my mind, agenda and calendar. I'm an only child to both my mother and father, but have very close friends, who I consider sisters since childhood. But, to be honest, I have always preferred to hang with the guys, who I easily bonded with. This book is an introduction and the first diary of a series full of inspiration, thoughts, raw emotions and lessons that I want to share with other girl moms, expecting moms and daughters. This book is also for my daughter, Clue Wilson, a book I wish my mother had read.

JUST A LITTLE HISTORY

My mother has eight sisters and brothers. I have heard stories from each one of my aunts and uncles, they collectively share stories of trauma and dysfunction in which I'm sure played a part with how they chose to parent their kids. My mother often expressed how my grandmother always kept a house and a man, but she was never stable. Everyone had a different father and a random last name, in fact, 'til this day I still don't know the nigga's whose last name I have. My mom spoke on how my grandmother would always be *"Locked up in the room"* (as she put it). I never saw having the doors locked as problematic, though I always heard much it bothered her, even as an adult. Now, I fully understand that it wasn't necessarily the locked doors that bothered her, but more so the concept of being unable to access her mother. My mother and her siblings would often come home and find their things thrown outside. One day, my mom and one of her sisters, who share the same father but not the same last name, ran away to be raised by their biological father and his wife. They clearly exposed her to another life because she spoke so highly of them and the way that they were brought up, compared to how their life was being with her mother. My grandmother had both a negative and positive influence on my mother's parenting. Though, I cannot say which person or household impacted what exact behavior or influenced certain ways of thinking as a mother. I can only talk about what I experienced and learned, both consciously and subconsciously.

THE FOUNDATION

What we start with as kids ultimately shapes who we become as adults. I believe that it is very important to self-reflect and look back on what you were taught as a child, because doing so will reveal all of the answers as to why and how you think the way that you do. I'm sure most parents have their child's best interest at heart and meant well through all of their teachings. However, some lessons were just traditional bullshit that was taught to them as a kid by an adult, they then continued to pass the bullshit on.

Looking back and replaying things in my head that I was told as a child, (not necessarily by my mother, but adults in general) I realize that most of it was senseless. Most of it couldn't even be explained by them, the teacher, because we weren't allowed to ask "why?"

It took me to become an adult to realize that not all parents are adults and not all adults are smart. I know that my mother always wanted the best for me. I was well kept, attended private schools, rode private transportation and always wore the latest trend. I had my own room, which was kind of a big deal back then, because everyone that I knew had brothers and sisters who shared everything. We kept a stable household. It was always very neat, clean and as an added bonus, I only knew of one man who I refer to as my dad, being that my biological dad passed away during my early childhood. The reason I called it a bonus is because this is one thing that I know my mother prided herself on, contrary to my grandmother. I was taught the basic fundamentals about being a young lady, how to conduct a household, how to look perfect, how to dress *Ladylike*, how to talk and how to be everything she wanted me to be or that she didn't have the chance to be. She taught me how to be everything, except myself.

I love my mother dearly, as I know she loves me. I know that she will always expect greatness from me and wants what she believes is best for me. So, this is not a jab at her parenting because I believe she did great and the best she could with what she was taught.

What I did not receive as a girl is emotional support, affection, the *"Okay"* to make mistakes or permission to express myself. This shaped the way I maneuvered through adolescence and adulthood.

After having my second son, I started paying attention to certain things I would do and say that I had always considered to be *"just who I am."* I began to challenge myself with questions like *"Is this really who I am?"* What I later realized is that you don't have to do everything that was done to you or carry the torch of bad habits and conditioning just because that's what momma, daddy, grandma, etc. had taught you. All of those things are just tradition and to me tradition is just the old way of doing things.

Every piece of information learned has an alternative. As you grow you should add to and update the notes so that you can evolve comfortably. It is okay to relearn certain shit, especially if the original lesson hasn't worked for anyone.

Reshaping your mind by unpacking childhood trauma and getting out of the habit of doing things that are familiar are both a part of breaking generational curses. This allows you to establish healthy relationships with yourself and your children. I am thirty-four years old and I am positive that I have broken so many chains with my sons, now having a daughter gives me extra wind.

This book is not a blueprint on "Perfect Patty" parenting because I am still learning, unlearning, recycling and throwing away lessons four (almost five) kids in. This is a reminder to you, myself and our children (especially our daughters) that they are not perfect and nor do they need to be. Everything written from this sentence forward is to encourage self-awareness and emotional stability, so that we can create positive, functional relationships with our kids.

THE MAKING OF A GIRL MOM

FEBRUARY 23, 2020

I keep a period tracker on my phone that I use, but really saw no need for it being that I was celibate for two whole damn years. I had an on again, off again relationship with someone who I will refer to as *"The Number Feaux."* Who did a two year prison sentence. During that time I had shifted my focus to full-time grind mode, simply because for me, sex involves an emotional connection and nobody kept my interest. We stayed together because casual sex wasn't even an option, this thing is way too good to have people entangled with me. That is how domestic violence starts. Anyways, he came home January 22, 2020 and because of my lack of action before, I wasn't in the habit of logging my menstruation properly. So I may have miscalculated my ovulation date. Previously, I would know it came down but wouldn't actually track it until the following week, typically once the app sent me a reminder. Most times I'd have to guess the dates, which most likely threw my entire calendar off by a few days. Also, I am big on herbs, natural products and remedies. Around the end of December, I did a "New Year" cleanse including yoni pearls and Maca Root. I usually do extensive research on what I put into my body, but I never considered how that helped my fertility. Feeling very normal, talking shit on the phone, I went to Walmart. Ironically, there were two women in line ahead of me who I noticed were purchasing pregnancy tests. I said to my friend on the phone *"What in the hell they got going on. Everybody is purchasing pregnancy tests."* With no intentions to, I made it to the register and asked out of the blue, *"Can I get the $10 test from back?"* I never planned on using it, but decided to make the impulsive purchase, plus I usually keep them on hand to be safe.

FEBRUARY 29, 2020

A reminder flashed across my phone screen *"Did you forget to track your period?"* This was normal for me to see because again I wasn't active and would just track it when I remembered. But, this time was different, panic set in. I called my sister, Redd, and texted my friend and business consultant, Jah, to express to them my stress levels of what could be. They both convinced me to take the test even though it was in the middle of the day. Anyone who has had a pregnancy scare knows that you should use first morning urine. I went ahead and took the test, a faint line appeared. *"Nahh, this shit can't be right because I didn't even use the right urine"* is what I kept telling myself. There were two tests in the box, so I took another one. The same ole dumb ass line appeared. I mean at this point, I don't even think I was seeing correctly, so I sent pictures to the testing lab (my support team). They both confirmed what I knew, that it was positive. What a fuckin' leap year. Nobody asked for an extra day in February.

MARCH 1, 2020

I'm up early in the morning, ready to bust the doors down at Walmart for a digital test because this two line thingy is saying all of the wrong shit. For some strange reason, when I thought that I wasn't pregnant, I bought the test with confidence. But, on this day I was nervous as hell and damn near dressed in drag at 8am. When I made it home, I tested immediately and it read. . . PREGNANT!

MARCH 11, 2020

Anxiety, stress, depression, sadness and panic in the middle of a pandemic is all that I can feel. My first thoughts were very negative given everything that I had been through with "The Number Feaux". On top of that I had made plans that were pretty much set in stone for the entire Spring and Summer, that were not going to be cancelled. Thoughts of how my kids were gonna feel trumped also ran through my head, along with all of the other things mentioned. My close friends and family, along with a few who have been a part of my intimate Instagram live chats know that I was diagnosed with mild depression and anxiety. I suffer from really bad panic attacks, mostly when I'm over thinking, so during this time, I was losing it. My thoughts were everywhere. I don't know how to open up and be vulnerable. It's difficult for me to be straight off the bat with my feelings in the midst of going through anything, especially involving my true emotions. I don't like for people to pity me, nor do I like to feel weak. However, I am emotional and I do cry just like you. But, I only breakdown after I have had time to myself to process everything alone. All I can think about is how bad the timing is. After all, I have two sons in high school, one in middle school and their fathers are deceased. I also have a younger son who is in elementary. So many questions were running through my head. *How will a newborn fit in with your lifestyle? You were married before, are you ready to do it again for the sake of the new kid on the block? Do you even wanna be in a relationship? Do you wanna take a chance co-parenting again? Look at how that's going for you now. You know you suffer with separation anxiety. What are people going to say? Think? Really? A single parent of five?* With all of these tabs open in my head, I scheduled an abortion appointment ASAP. I was given an appointment that following Friday, which would have made me about nine weeks at the time of visit. They sent me a message to confirm the date 48 hours before and I was set.

MARCH 13, 2020

Still nervous and indecisive, the doctor's office sent me a cancellation text. At the time I didn't know why, but I now know it was due to preparation for COVID. *Okay, is this a sign from God? Is this an excuse to move forward even though I'm still unsure?* Those were the conversations I had with myself.

MARCH 16, 2020

Three days go by, I'm overwhelmed with emotions, thoughts, sickness, and senseless arguments that constantly pushed my decision needle over the "FUCK NO" meter. So I Googled and found another clinic with the same name as the first one who cancelled my appointment, just a different location. Crazy enough, they scheduled me for the very next day.

MARCH 17, 2020

I'm up early dressed and ready for my day. I even took my prescribed Xanax just to calm my body. This day was hands down the most emotional, self reflecting day I had experienced in a long time. So, I walked into the office and the very first thing that I noticed was that everyone there was an elder. They were overly nice and made sure that I was comfortable while I sat and waited for my name to be called. The entire setting reminded me of a church. Looking back, I might've been the only patient that stayed the entire time. Once I was called to the back a

younger lady with a belly performed an ultrasound on me. Quickly after, they ushered me into another room where two older ladies sat waiting with pen, pad and Bible. Initially I thought to myself *"Okay, this must be the part where they confirm my decision concerning the abortion."* Based on my understanding, before scheduling the actual procedure, you must take part in counseling and signing of legal documents. Wrong!! As soon as I sat down, they asked if I would mind if we started with a prayer. Shit, I was thinking to myself, *Ma'am I don't give a fuck what you start with because in all honesty*

I talk to God everyday, all day and I am sure that He has heard everything that I had to say thus far. Yet, here we are. But, if this was gonna help move the process along, hell, I even woulda led us. We prayed, then I sat there while they interrogated me. Although I am a firm believer in God, I am also a believer of Pro-Choice. I was very nonchalant at first. When I realized this meeting wasn't going as I expected, I actually started thinking about the questions they were asking. Once I found myself in deep thought in the midst of it, I knew I needed to regain control. I clearly stated that I was not interested in continuing this pregnancy. I had to make it clear in case they had missed that part. That's when the one holding the clipboard and Bible looked dead into my eyes and said *"Oh baby we don't do that here because this is a Christian facility."* Luckily, I had taken my meds because if I hadn't, I know at that point I would've lost it. After all, I'm about ten weeks pregnant and was not interested in having the surgical procedure (which would have been required if I waited too much longer). I was only considering the pill option. Respectfully I asked, *"Isn't this Planned Parenthood?"* She said *"Yes, but we're privately *funded."* Summore Shit I thought. At this point I was pretty much over the entire day and it was only noon, but I sat and listened anyway. The most important questions that stuck out to me were: *Who makes the decisions for you and your kids? Do you want anymore kids? If so, when is the right time for you? Are you financially stable? How would the father feel being that this would be his first child. Does what other people think about you play a part in your decision making?* These were some real Prayer Warriors. The assistant warrior sat quietly for the majority of the meeting and observed. We awkwardly locked eyes a few times as I began to check my Apple watch religiously. I wasn't trying to be rude, but I was contemplating on getting home so that I could absorb everything that had happened. On top of that, I was suffering from morning sickness. As the warrior in charge concluded with closing remarks and statements, the assistant asked me to take a walk with her before I left. She reminded me of my great-grandmother. She led me to a back room where there were countless baby items. It looked like a mini baby store. She explained to me their programs and resources, none of it included information about what I came for. She spoke very few words, but they were way more meaningful than everything that I had heard today aside from the twenty-one questions. It was her tone, her spirit and her firm hug that filled me with emotions. She spoke to me like she knew me, by only the few words I had used to answer the questions that were asked earlier. I felt like she understood all of the things that I didn't say. She grabbed me as I was leaving and hugged me so long and tight. As I came up for air, wiping my eyes, she asked if she could give me a gift. I said *"yeah"* and stood there shocked as she put a pink set of crocheted baby booties, hat, mittens and socks in my hand. Which was ironic, because I had never mentioned that I had all boys, nor had I told her that if I had a way of knowing what I was having that would also be a determining factor. She also slipped me her personal contact information, along with a packet listing doctors that I never really planned to use. Once I made it to the parking lot I inhaled and exhaled deeply as I sat in my car for about five minutes trying to regroup. Feeling even more confused and indecisive than when I came, I searched in my Google history for another abortion clinic. I also used the list I was just given to schedule a doctor's appointment as well.

MARCH 18, 2020

It had been four long weeks until my scheduled appointments and I am ready to get it over with. Originally, I was only willing to use the abortion pill, but I was now ready to recant that statement. I had a lot going on. During this time "The Number Feaux" had came back from New Orleans, the boys were out of school because of the pandemic and I actually thought that I would die from morning sickness. The fact that we were all pretty much stuck together all day hearing "Ma," on top of homeschooling a six-year-old, was sending me. Also, every time I had a disagreement with "The Number Feaux" (which was most likely every five minutes if I had to count), I would reflect. I think I spent each moment weighing out the same shit over and over again. Shedrick (my oldest and adopted son), his mother and I had some urgent business to take care of in New Orleans. I was now fifteen weeks pregnant, both appointments were scheduled a few days away and two days apart. So I jumped on the road, since flying wasn't advised, got the business handled and rushed back.

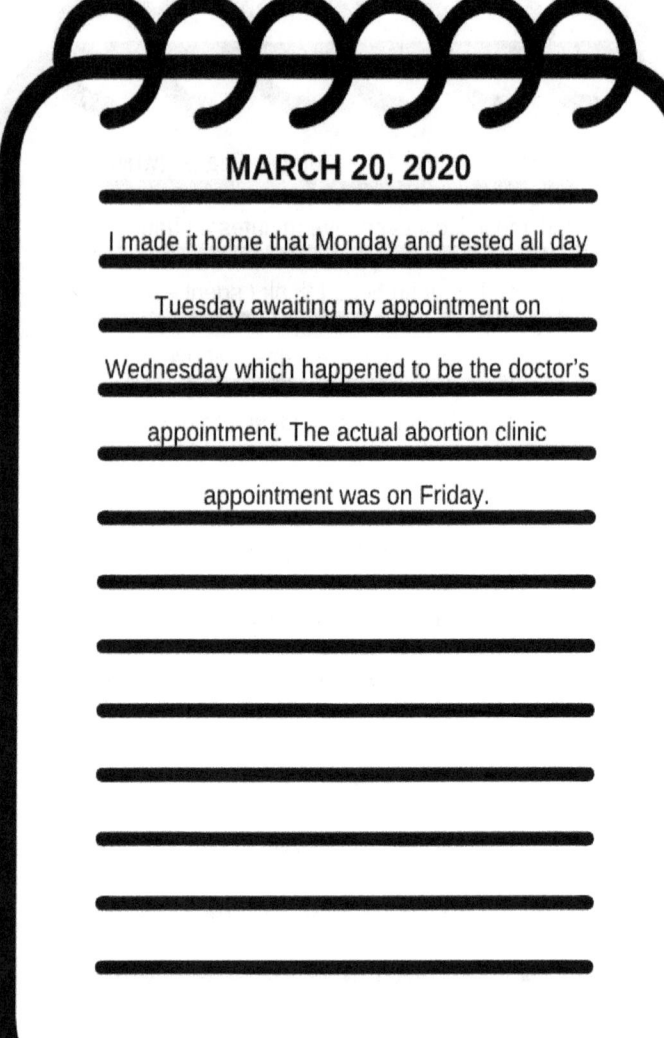

MARCH 20, 2020

I made it home that Monday and rested all day Tuesday awaiting my appointment on Wednesday which happened to be the doctor's appointment. The actual abortion clinic appointment was on Friday.

MARCH 22, 2020

I checked in, then filled out all kinds of "unnecessary" paperwork. They quickly called my name and directed me to another part of the building, into a dark room where an ultrasound tech stood waiting. She lathered my belly with warm jelly and she played the heartbeat, measured body parts, then asked if I would like to know what I was having. I laughed to myself like "Bitch is this a trick question?" But, outloud all I said was "yeah, sure!" That's when I heard the three magic words "It's a girl" and went completely deaf. She printed me about seven ultrasound pictures for keepsakes, with her legs wide open with the words "It's a girl" typed in between. I couldn't get out of the office quick enough before I took a photo of the ultrasound and sent it to my son's group chat, "The Number Feaux," my select family group and my original support team (Red, Tori, Jah and Flay). Later that day I sent it to my momma. My mother happened to be last to be contacted simply because I dreaded what she would say the most. I had to prepare myself mentally and emotionally for whatever she would say. In the black community, having a baby is almost one of the worst things that a woman can do at first. No matter how successful she's viewed, it's an issue then after a while it's all good. That's some real psychological bullshit. However, to my surprise everyone was overjoyed and excited for me. I, on the other hand, was overwhelmed. After receiving the approval of my family I immediately felt better, it was like a weight was lifted off of my shoulders and I didn't even feel sick anymore. Oftentimes, we tend to boldly boast about how grown we are and how we don't care about what people think about us but most times it's a facade. At that very moment the relief I felt confirmed that I did care about what others thought. Specifically, those that I sent that initial text to, but I definitely could've lived with everyone's rejection or opinions but my sons. I didn't have that to worry about though because they were already in the group chat thinking of names and talking about things that they couldn't wait to teach her. Her father was elated, feeling as though he had finally "won" a battle with me I'm sure. My mother came up with the name "Clue" a few days later and it stuck.

MARCH 24, 2020

Needless to say, Friday came and I had forgot all about that stupid, senseless appointment because I knew wtf I was doing. Suddenly everything came together and started to make sense. The canceled appointments, the prayer warriors, the pink gift, the rescheduling and arrangements of the doctor's appointment and also the pandemic. With the pandemic being very serious and dangerous, it worked out to be a blessing to me. My schedule was canceled because of it and not because I was pregnant. Of course some things are still unexplainable

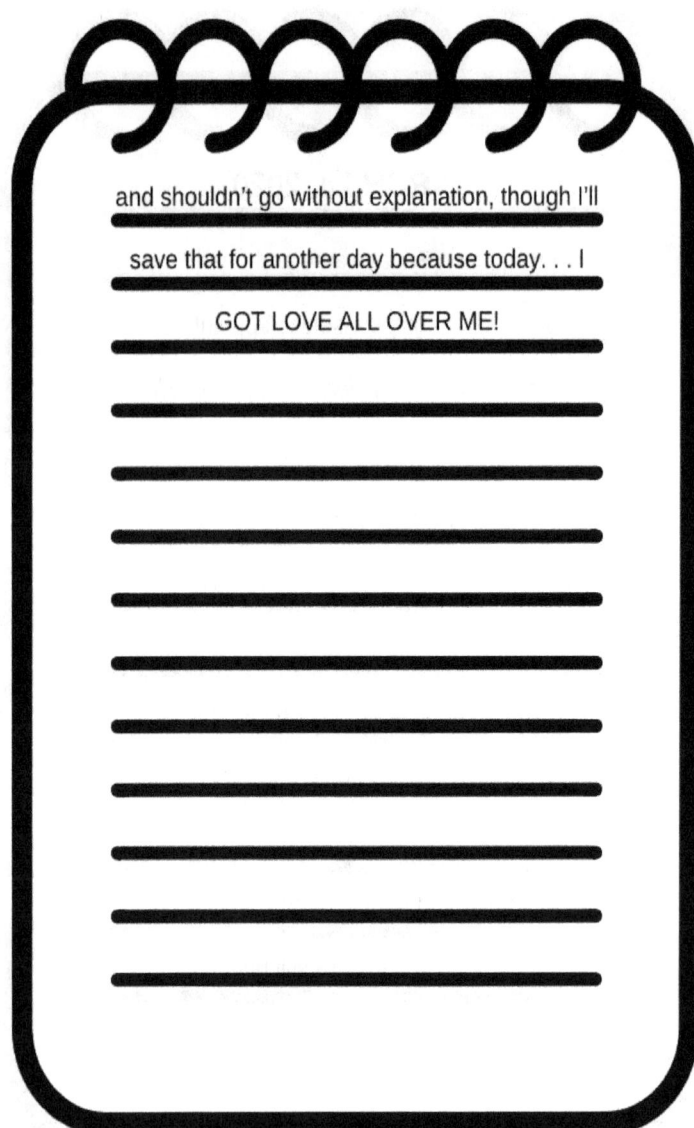

and shouldn't go without explanation, though I'll save that for another day because today. . . I GOT LOVE ALL OVER ME!

THE BEGINNING OF ACCEPTANCE

In these times of the internet, we have all fallen victim to sharing details of our personal lives too soon and in exchange we are bombarded with unwanted advice and opinions. In reference to pregnancy, we get opinions about what we should and should not eat, drink, wear and do. This can become so overwhelming because all of a sudden everybody is an expert at knowing what's best for you. With the exception of experience, pregnancy is more so about you and your relationship with a brand-new human. This is a one of a kind experience no matter how many kids you have and should be treated as such.

Everyone doesn't have the same beliefs. Therefore, I decided to protect my energy and do things the way I wanted to, unrestricted, instead of moving to other people's beat whom I don't even know. I don't want or care to make sense of anybody else's life but my own. I'm only interested in meeting my own expectations. Pregnancy is a good time to form a bond with your baby and reflect on lessons you were taught, as well as lessons you want to teach.

Being a social media personality and public figure, I often see posts about marriage and relationships. Most aren't based on reality but are solely based on what someone else told them. This, of course, is unrealistic to apply general rules and regulations to relationships, when every individual requires and desires different things to thrive. Being married before and divorced, I am still optimistic about love and marriage, though my views have since changed. I realized that I did a lot of things prematurely, because I wasn't doing what I felt, but instead was doing what I was taught.

Since then, I have changed my focus. Although I was raised on the Bible, I now focus more on relationships with God than religion, so I don't feel like marriage is an actual goal for me anymore. I also don't feel like anyone should be married before having kids nor should they stay in a marriage or relationship for the sake of kids. If the kids don't get to see you all function as a healthy family, what is the sense of it? I mean, after all, I waited for marriage to have Blaze and thought everything was perfect, until it wasn't.

Marriage does not predict the outcome of a relationship. You can be the one he marries and still not be happy. You can be the one he marries and still be played and mistreated. It's normal for people to outgrow each other and fall out of love. What good is a title if the feelings don't match? What good is it to broadcast and boast about a relationship that does nothing for you? Is it just to be able to say that you were/are married? How does that serve you if it's not all love? I'll be thirty-five this year, *The Number Feaux* on the other hand is only thirty with not much experience with relationships or his own kids, he was more interested in marriage than me.

I'm more hesitant and cautious simply because I have a bigger picture to reference being that I've been there and done that. Parents can be gay, straight, bisexual, married, straight or single these days. What matters most is the emotional well-being of the child in relation to the parents relationship. I only reserve the most peaceful roads when choosing any relationship because the past usually always comes back to kick us in the ass and sometimes our children too.

    I believe that it's not family structure that matters most, it's how we all feel about each other and get along. Regardless of the status of her father and I, Clue will know that she was made from love (despite the emotions I shuffled through to get here) and that is more important than any title anyone can give.

WHAT IS LOVE?

I think that everyone has their own definition of what love truly means to them. For me love is respect, protectiveness, sincerity, free, unconditional, compassion and empathy. It cannot be bought, manipulated or sold. Love is the foundation of any relationship, but most importantly any mother/child relationship. As a mother, you are your child's first teacher. A baby comes from the womb and relies on our nature and their environment for his/her needs. Which means we, as parents, have a huge influence over them.

We get ideas of what a parent should be by watching our parents, other parents and reading books/watching TV. As young mothers, we focus on so many big lessons that we want to teach our kids, that we tend to forget about the smaller and most important lessons. My goal is to instill in my baby a secure attachment bond. Every bond is a little different whether it's complicated, needy, or just loving. In relation to my childhood experience, I can't say that I had a secure bond. I do however identify with it being complicated. This is what I will continue to avoid. Children learn by example. I remember hearing *"Do as I say, not as I do"* often. As a kid this was such a confusing lesson. How can I do something that I have no experience in, nor seen in demonstration to do it correctly?

RAISING YOUR SONS & DAUGHTERS EQUALLY

Already having four sons and now bringing in a girl into this world, I want to make sure that I raise them equally. Although there's an obvious gap in age, the rules will be built on the same foundation. I want all of my children to be happy and successful. Most mothers are more lenient and understanding with their sons all in the name of *"they're just being boys."*

Mothers tend to be more protective and stricter with their daughters, which usually gives them no room for fuckups or mistakes. Girls are taught early (even when there's an older brother in the house) how to cook, clean, do laundry and how to be the overall responsible one. I have even seen some girls take on the role of "momma" when she's not home. Though, sons get to be wild and free, with maybe one house assignment which is to take out the trash. We also raise our sons to be more hard body, lack emotion, be strong, straight faced and protective individuals early on.

I don't think any good parent intends to treat their kids differently just because of their gender. I think that is what society has taught us to do. All of our stereotypical beliefs will influence our kids' beliefs about their own abilities. The old saying is *"Girls mature faster than boys,"* but I believe whatever you water, will grow.

In my house, everyone starts out with the exact same trust. The ages in dating and "How To" rules will be no different because I have the exact same expectation for my kids. I won't put the fear of becoming pregnant on my daughter simply because she's a girl when obviously it takes two genders to create a life. All children should be protected, cared for and treated equally because that is how we stop raising overqualified women and underqualified men and vice versa. Everyone should be taught the same set of rules, with a little tweaking based on the individual, so that it is easier when they are ready to date, marry and have kids.

I was raised in the 90's and was taught to always keep my own everything and to never depend on anyone. The men that I have dated were taught to provide but not do much for themselves. Meaning they might work and do the things that men were taught to do for women, but always needed help to get things done for themselves. For example: A house. Most men don't think they need a house without a woman because they have been conditioned to believe that women take care of the house. They usually go from living at momma's house to their girlfriend/wife's home and when things don't work out, back to momma's house or on to another girlfriend.

While on the other hand, women (with the exception of those who were taught to scout men for security) are taught to create our own stability. Men are wants not needs. This is why I teach my sons everything that I know. They will know how to cook, clean, do every chore, provide for themselves first, protect and express themselves emotionally (without feeling weak). Clue will be no different. The rules are the rules.

FEAUX REASONS CLUE WILL NOT BE CLUELESS

SHARING THE THINGS I WISH I HEARD AS A CHILD

1.) YOU ARE NEVER TOO MUCH. YOU WERE CREATED IN GOD'S EYE AND YOU ARE FULLY EQUIPPED TO BE YOURSELF. YOU WERE BEAUTIFULLY AND WONDERFULLY MADE, THERE IS NOTHING ABOUT YOU THAT IS WRONG. YOU

ONLY HAVE ROOM TO GROW INTO A BIGGER AND BETTER YOU. I DON'T EXPECT YOU TO BE ANYONE BUT YOURSELF, NOR WILL I EVER SEE A COMPARISON TO YOU CLUE BECAUSE YOU ARE YOU. UNDERSTAND THAT DIFFERENT IS COOL. NO MATTER WHAT NORMAL IS TO ANYONE ELSE, ALWAYS KNOW THAT YOU CREATE YOUR OWN NORMAL. THEY CAN'T BE YOU AND YOU

CAN'T BE THEM. THIS IS AN ADVANTAGE THAT YOU WILL ALWAYS HAVE OVER EVERYTHING. FUCK WHO DON'T LIKE YOU.

2.) NO IS NOT A BAD WORD. YOUR FEELINGS ARE IMPORTANT TO ME SO BE HONEST ABOUT WHAT YOU FEEL EVEN IF YOU THINK NO ONE IS LISTENING. IT IS OKAY TO NOT WANT TO. YOU CAN CHANGE YOUR

MIND WHENEVER YOUR BODY AND SPIRIT TELLS YOU TO. IT'S OKAY TO ASK QUESTIONS BEFORE YOU SAY YES. ALWAYS LISTEN TO YOUR BODY'S RESPONSE TO PEOPLE AND FEEL FREE TO USE YOUR EMOTIONS TO SET YOUR BOUNDARIES. YOU ARE A CHILD, BUT YOUR FEELINGS ARE VALID AND WILL ALWAYS BE RESPECTED. I HEAR YOUR LIKES, DISLIKES AND YOUR

SILENCE. YOU SHOULD ALWAYS FEEL SAFE, SO NEVER IGNORE HOW YOU FEEL FOR ANYONE, BIG SMALL, YOUNG OR OLD. RESPECTFULLY, I ALWAYS GOT YOUR BACK.

3.) IT'S OKAY TO GET IT WRONG. LEARNING IS A CONTINUOUS LIFE PROCESS. YOU CAN'T CONTROL EVERY OUTCOME BECAUSE NOTHING AND NO

ONE IS PERFECT. SEEK CLARITY ON WHAT YOU DO NOT UNDERSTAND. MAKE NOISE, USE YOUR CREATIVITY AND IMAGINATION. EVERYTHING DOESN'T NEED TO BE DONE MY WAY, BECAUSE I CAN'T WAIT TO LEARN THINGS FROM YOU. BE TEACHABLE. BE VULNERABLE. I STILL MAKE MISTAKES IN MY OLD AGE AND AS YOUR MOTHER. MISTAKES ARE WHAT MAKES

YOU WISE WHEN YOU LEARN FROM THEM. THAT'S WHY I WILL ALWAYS DO MY BEST, NO MATTER HOW HARD IT MAY BE, TO SHARE AND SHOW MY SHORTCOMINGS AND MY WRONGS. I WILL ALSO ALWAYS SHARE MY SUCCESS AND MY RIGHTS. MISTAKES ARE APART OF WHO WE ARE AND WHO WE WILL BE. JUST BECAUSE YOU GOT IT WRONG DOESN'T MEAN THAT

YOU'RE A FAILURE, NO MATTER WHO'S WATCHING. YOU ARE BUILT FOR WHATEVER GIRL.

4.) I LOVE YOU.

IT'S FUNNY BECAUSE THESE THREE WORDS, NO MATTER HOW DEEPLY FELT HAVE ALWAYS MADE ME FEEL UNCOMFORTABLE. HUGS AND KISSES WAS ALSO NEVER MY LOVE LANGUAGE. HOWEVER, I'VE BEEN

PRACTICING JUST FOR YOU AND WILL SHOWER YOU WITH AFFECTION AS YOUR BROTHERS HAVE SHOWN ME. I DON'T NEED YOU TO JUST HEAR THOSE WORDS. I WANT YOU TO FEEL THOSE WORDS NO MATTER WHERE YOU ARE SO THAT NO ONE CAN TELL YOU DIFFERENT. WHEN YOU HEAR ME SAY "I LOVE YOU" I PRAY YOU FEEL ENCOURAGED, MOTIVATED, TRUSTED, AT PEACE,

SECURE AND CONFIDENT. WITH A DAD LIKE YOURS, FOUR BROTHERS AND A BAD ASS MOMMY LIKE MYSELF... LOVE IS ONE THING YOU WON'T EVER LACK MISS CLUE. WE LOVE YOU!

CONCLUSION

As a mother, you will always be a reflection of your child in some form or fashion. Much of what they think and how they feel about themselves is influenced by how we feel about ourselves, starting during pregnancy. Our kids do as they are done and not as they are told. Therefore, we should always be conscious of the way we treat them, relate to them and bond with them. I find common ground with my kids by thinking back on what I felt like as a child, along with therapy. Thinking of this can help us become more aware of the reason we act the way we do towards our child(ren). Although kids tend to mimic their parents, as children grow older they develop their own personality. This is why it is important to listen and encourage love and authenticity. The transfer of information happens through everyday interaction. Either we fall into the roles of what our parents demonstrated, or we create our own. We may even blend ours and theirs together or be the total opposite. It's up to you to make that conscious decision.

To those women who may be struggling to come to a decision on whether or not you should bring a new life into this world, DO WHAT YOU WANT TO DO. Don't allow others to put their opinions and fears on you. While every child deserves a chance to experience a relationship with their father, do not be discouraged if things don't work out. It's true that we tend to ignore red flags, but we also cannot predict the future. Focus on you and become the best mother you can be regardless of the title or status of a relationship. Whether you're blessed with a boy or girl they both require the exact same foundation from you.

I believe that our children are a reflection of the part of us that did not heal. The last thing we want to do as mothers is to pass on childhood traumas consciously or subconsciously. Let's focus more on healing through listening and understanding rather than control. I wrote this book for me and those who may share some of the same experiences that I have. With self-reflection and honesty, I hope that my truth helps encourage self-awareness and promotes emotional stability, to create positive, functional relationships with your kids.

www.ingramcontent.com/pod-product-compliance
Lightning Source LLC
Chambersburg PA
CBHW070059100426
42743CB00012B/2598